ADULT

LEADER GUIDE

A Study of Luther's Small Catechism for Adults

by Eugene C. Kreider

Augsburg Fortress
Minneapolis

Contents

A STUDY OF LUTHER'S SMALL CATECHISM FOR ADULTS
Lutheran Faith and Life Series
Adult Leader Guide

This Leader Guide is for use with the Adult Student Book

Thomas S. Hanson and Carolyn F. Lystig, editors
RKB Studios, inside designer
Gary Baune/Hetland, Ltd., cover artwork
Koechel Peterson and Associates, Inc., logo and cover design

Scripture quotations are from the New Revised Standard Version Bible, copyright © 1989, Division of
Christian Education of the National Council of Churches of Christ in the United States of America.
Used by permission.

Introduction

SERIES OVERVIEW

A *Study of Luther's Small Catechism for Adults* is part of the Lutheran Faith and Life Series. This series presents the Lutheran heritage of the Evangelical Lutheran Church in America to children, youth, and adults. The resources in this series reinforce the Lutheran traditions of reverence for God's Word, faithfulness in worship, and understanding of Martin Luther's Small Catechism. As students and teachers remember the heritage and spiritual life of their denomination and their congregation, they will be challenged to move into the future with a renewed sense of mission and outreach.

Luther's Small Catechism offers both a study of history and a look at contemporary life. It comes out of 16th century Germany and was written by Martin Luther (A.D. 1483–1546) for people in his time. It reflects his thinking about the essentials of the Christian faith and gathers up the witness of Christians through the ages. From that perspective, we study the Small Catechism as a piece of history. But in so doing, we discover that the faith it speaks about is our faith, too. Luther's Small Catechism is part of the foundation of our past for our life of faith today.

Luther wrote the Small Catechism for adults to use in their own faith development and as a tool for helping them teach the young. He took five key elements from historical Christian experience (the Ten Commandments, the Apostles' Creed, the Lord's Prayer, Baptism, and the Lord's Supper), plus a concern for the setting of communal church life in the present, and turned them all into educational experiences.

A study of heritage defines the educational task in a certain way. It makes the subject matter the living faith of those in the past and learning a matter of looking intently and openly at their faithfulness. That is the most important thing we learn from our heritage—the faithfulness of God. We teach that to others the way it was taught to us— by witnessing to a living relationship with God.

Luther fostered this concern for learning and living the heritage of faith through the use of questions for personal reflection and discussion. In that way, the faith of the past could come alive in the present.

In reality, heritage is something that keeps growing and building. As we get to know it, what it means for us, and then live it, we take part in that creative enterprise. What we do with heritage in our lives will be what we give to the next generation. It will be a living heritage if it comes out of our own wrestling with what we have received rather than being just a word for word handing over of the information from the past. Our heritage reflects how we have put Luther's teachings into practice through our congregations and national church bodies.

SERIES GOALS

The goals of the Lutheran Faith and Life Series are to help teachers and students:
- learn about and celebrate their Lutheran heritage at all ages of life;
- develop a sense of appreciation of the heritage of the Lutheran church and treasure it within their Christian faith;
- respond to God's grace with lives of faithfulness to God and service to others.

USING THE SERIES RESOURCES

Lutheran Faith and Life resources can be used as a teaching and learning resource for: weekday classes; family night; home use; longer and later confirmation classes; camping and retreats; summer programs; Christian day schools; youth groups; choirs; and Sunday morning programs. Detailed information and helps for using Lutheran Faith and Life in these settings can be found in the planning guide for this series. Before you begin planning the sessions you will teach, make sure you have information about the setting for teaching, the number of times your class will meet, and the amount of time scheduled for each class period.

COURSE OVERVIEW AND OBJECTIVES

A *Study of Luther's Small Catechism for Adults* will introduce the participants to Luther's Small Catechism as one of the foundation stones of the Lutheran expression of the Christian faith. Study of the Small Catechism will help the participants gain a clearer understanding of the good news of God's decision to save them in Jesus Christ and of their call to be witnesses to that good news in their daily lives.

The course is divided into an introduction and six chapters. Chapters 1–5 discuss the chief parts of the Small Catechism (the Ten Commandments, the Apostles' Creed, the Lord's Prayer, the Sacrament of Holy Baptism, and the Sacrament of the Lord's Supper). Chapter 6 discusses what Luther called the seven marks or characteristics of the Christian church (the Word of God, Baptism, the Lord's Supper, confession and absolution, the ministry, worship, and suffering.)

The overall goals for this six-chapter study are to provide an opportunity for adults to:

■ become acquainted or reacquainted with the essentials of the Christian faith;

■ encounter and be challenged by Luther's Small Catechism as a source for deepening their personal faith;

■ see the intersection of the Christian faith and their lives and explore ways to practice that faith daily.

The most likely audiences for this study will be:

1. those entering instruction into the Christian faith, especially those who are not from Lutheran backgrounds;

2. those who want to renew or refresh their understanding of Lutheran theology, faith, and life;

3. adult baptismal candidates;

4. parents of children being baptized or beginning confirmation instruction.

COURSE MATERIALS

The basic materials for this course are the study book and this leader guide. In addition, participants are encouraged to use their Bibles during the study. The Bible translation suggested for this course is the New Revised Standard Version (NRSV).

This leader guide contains background information and instructions for leading the study. This guide explains how to use the study book and also provides many other suggestions to encourage learning and further exploration. You will find it helpful in preparing for each class session. You will need to plan ahead on how the study book will be used.

Although this course is arranged in six chapters, the study book and this guide are designed to allow the study of each chapter to be expanded over two or more class sessions.

The study book contains Luther's Small Catechism and commentary on each part. Each participant will need a copy of the study book. The study book is intended to be consulted and reread by the participant long after the course is ended.

LEADER GUIDE FORMAT

The format of this course has three parts that are briefly described below. The format makes ses-

sion preparation easy to organize the basic session plan in easy-to-follow steps.

PRE-STUDY

This section provides the introductory information needed to plan and lead the class sessions.
Focus statement. The focus of each chapter summarizes the main theme of each chapter.
Chapter objectives. The specific learning objectives are provided for each chapter.
Background. This section provides additional theological and education background information on the parts of the Small Catechism and on the Christian faith and may be shared with the participants.
Materials list. This list indicates all the items needed for teaching the session.
Before the study. Read this section to learn what basic preparations should be made prior to class time.

STUDY

This section provides directions and materials for teaching the chapter. Remember that each chapter may be expanded over two or more class periods. You will need to make choices on which activities you feel will be most helpful and will work best with your group in your situation. Each chapter of this guide is divided into five major parts: "Entry," "Exploring the Study Book," "Digging Deeper," "For Reflection," and "Our Prayers."

Entry. This section refers the participants to the opening paragraphs of the chapter in the study book. By reading these paragraphs and reflecting on them, the participants enter into the central theme of the chapter.

Exploring the study book. This section contains two parts: "Reading the . . ." and "Key Points to Consider." Under "Reading the . . . ," participants are introduced to the text of the Small Catechism studied in the chapter. Together with the commentary, discussion questions, and Bible references, the participants encounter the Catechism and God's word that proceeds from it. Under "Key Points to Consider," important concepts and ideas of the chapter are highlighted for the leader. You will want to make extensive use of these suggestions if you are allotting only one class period for each chapter.

Digging deeper. This section includes a wide variety of activities and uses a number of teaching methods to present the participants with information pertinent to the chapter. It also provides ways to integrate the daily faith and life experiences of the participants.

For reflection. This section is in both this guide and in the study book. The questions and statements in this section of the study book provide another point of entry and reflection on the meaning of the Small Catechism for the faith and life of the participants.

Our prayers. This section in both the study book and this guide provides suggestions for closing worship prayer. Hymns from *Lutheran Book of Worship* are suggested for use. It is also suggested that prayers be used from *Prayers Based on Luther's Small Catechism* (Augsburg Fortress, 1991), a companion book to this study.

POST-STUDY

Following the session, the leader needs to continue planning for future learning.

Expanding the session. This section provides additional ideas for expanding the learning outside of regular classroom settings. Suggestions for individual or class projects, guest speakers, and other activities are provided.

Looking ahead. This section alerts the leader to upcoming activities that may require more time to prepare or arrange. It also reminds the leader to inform the participants of what they are to read or do in preparation for the next session.

LEARNER AND LEADER

Adults who will use this resource represent a wide range of age and experience. We must not fall into the trap of assuming that all adults are somehow alike. In addition to knowing something about the potential represented by different ages, the leader must get to know individuals well enough to appreciate what each one brings to the learning from personal experience. Knowing the learner in terms of age-level differences and differences among individuals is an important principle of teaching.

Yet, in speaking of the adult learner, there are some general things that can be said that will be helpful. These generalities must, however, always be used to begin the process of knowing the individual learner and not considered as conclusions by which all learners can be understood.

Attention to the social and emotional development in the adult years is important. The struggles to balance the positive and negative events in their lives are just as real in adulthood as in earlier years. Factors of cultural differences and emotional and social development are especially critical in matters of faith because of the personal and group commitments they call forth. Those factors account for much of adult behavior in relationships in families, among friends, and in the workplace.

Adults have reached the stage of intellectual development in which they can think abstractly. This skill is important as adults consider their faith, but they have to be encouraged and supported in using it. For example, applying what is believed to daily life involves complex decisions that cannot be easily made or sustained. Small and large group discussions, as suggested in this study, will help foster thinking skills. As these discussions are used, it will be best to keep them focused on the questions of faith rather than to use them as quick paths to simple answers.

Adults like to be involved in the way they learn. Those who will lead this course can build on that desire by helping adults recognize and claim their needs and interests and by giving them opportunities to guide their own learning. Developing a climate of trust in the classroom is essential for such teaching and learning. The leader can best serve here by encouraging differences in faith commitments and by offering a supportive classroom atmosphere in which they can be expressed.

This does not mean making one's faith intensely private, but to provide opportunities for individuals to come to an awareness of their own personal faith in the context of the community of faith.

The formulation and living of one's faith needs practice. Discussions of the Small Catechism can be a place to plan action in the world as well as to reflect upon the essentials of Christian teaching.

Evelyn and James Whitehead assert that the two great gifts of our religious adulthood are conscience and charisms. They claim that as adults use these gifts, it must be admitted that no one has all the answers and that discerning courses of action in church and world requires listening publicly to other community voices ("Reviews for Religious," May–June, 1990).

THE LEARNING SETTING

The classroom space is not nearly as important to the learning experience as is the classroom environment. Try to create a warm, positive, welcoming environment that will encourage people to share their thoughts and ideas. A good way to do this is to involve the participants in planning and arranging the classroom setting.

Always keep supplies readily available. Plan ahead for such problems as broken pencils or a shortage of Bibles or study books.

You may want to meet as a class outside of the traditional classroom setting. This course can easily be taught in a home or a retreat setting. Such locations may help the participants see that the Small Catechism is not a course to be learned, but that it can serve as a guide for faith and life.

CHAPTER 1

Ten words of life

FOCUS STATEMENT

The Ten Commandments are not restrictions for their own sake—"shoulds," "oughts," "no-nos." God gave them as words of life for our sake.

OBJECTIVES

This chapter will help adults:

- learn more about the Ten Commandments as biblical foundations for faith;
- gain a new appreciation of the importance of the Ten Commandments in daily life;
- seek ways to live under the Ten Commandments to the fullest.

 **PRE-STUDY**

Background: The Ten Commandments

How do Lutherans consider the Ten Commandments and all of God's laws? That is an important question. For Luther, the law was never a means of justification. From the very beginning it was God who justified people by faith. (See Romans 4 and Galatians 3.) This justifying faith is not our work, but God's work given in us through the word (Romans 10:5-13).

The law was given for two other reasons. First, the law controls the old self within us—the sinful self—to keep the world in order. God's law was given so that people and nations could make laws to preserve peace and to establish justice. God's law protects us and commands that all people receive just care and treatment.

Second, the law was given to drive us to the promise—redemption through Jesus Christ. This is God's "strange work," as Luther called it. When God justifies freely, God pushes us to the conclusion that God alone can justify. We cannot rely on ourselves, on our obedience, or on our faith for salvation. We are totally dependent upon the promise given through Jesus' death and resurrection.

Some Lutherans began to speak of a third use or function of the law, although it is not clear whether Luther himself did or not. The third use of the law is the understanding that the law and the Ten Commandments function as a guide for life. Through the law, as embodied in the Ten Commandments, God shows us how we can live as God's people and as sister and brothers, one to another. It is this third use of the law on which this chapter focuses.

One of the things that comes to mind when we think of the Ten Commandments is the law—rules and regulations to live by. Sometimes the law is viewed negatively, as setting limits on the way we live. When that happens, the best we can hope for is that rules and regulations will help keep us from harming ourselves and others.

The Ten Commandments do set limits on the way we live. But the emphasis in each is positive. Under the third use, God gave the law to show us how life can be lived to the fullest. The Ten Commandments are not restrictions for their own sake—"shoulds," "oughts," or "no-nos." God gave them as words of life for our sake.

In every age, the Ten Commandments have offered the people of God realistic glimpses of life in its heights and depths. They show us the broad strokes of God's imaginative will as they reveal what life can be like according to the richness of creation.

Our life is caught between these glimpses and the promises of creation. We want wholeness, *shalom*, or at least a balance between what we know life to be and what we believe life can become. The Ten Commandments lead us to the place where we can look for that balance. They challenge us to look at life through them, as through a prism. As such, they are not a rule book or a guarantee of anything. Rather, as the third use of the law, they are a guide to continue searching for the best in life for ourselves, other people, and the rest of creation.

The Ten Commandments, as they have been taught and learned throughout history, have never been simply reduced to a list of divine "shoulds" or even to the best that laws can offer to keep the created world intact. There has been some of both. Even more, we have come to know the Ten Commandments as part of God's continuing, creative process in the world. As the third use, they are ten fundamental challenges to life in, through, and under God.

The commentary for this chapter in the study book speaks about this challenge in two ways that will be very helpful in this session and in the rest of the course. First, a study of the Ten Commandments inevitably calls upon us to develop some attitude toward our heritage and what it has to say about life today. Second, learning from our heritage is not a case of learning answers to the questions of faith and life that cannot be discussed or debated. Our faith heritage is a source to help us sharpen our own questions about what God means in life.

It is important to recognize that our religious heritage does not always tell us about life with God in straight forward statements or simple definitions. Many times what is said is in the form of a confession or statement of belief. For example, instead of claiming that the trouble and misfortune in life must be seen as expressions of God's love, regardless of what human experience has been, our heritage of faith claims that beyond all such experience, we can trust the steadfast love of God because of God's promises. Such a way of speaking does not define God's love by equating it with times of suffering. It is a confession of God's love beyond all the uncertainties of life.

These concerns are common matters for any course dealing with the heritage of faith. Significantly, they emerge with particular poignancy in this first chapter. It is not enough, as the study book states, to see the Ten Commandments in their simple application to life. They reach beyond that to the one who gave them and to the certainties of the relationship God established with humankind in Jesus Christ—the end of the law.

As Lutherans, we boldly confess that God's law, as embodied in the Ten Commandments, convicts us of our sinfulness and drives us solely to Christ for salvation. This is primary. Moving on from that, the primary questions we confront in this chapter are: "How do we take the beliefs and confessions of God and use them as ways of living in Christ in our world today?" and "How can the Ten Commandments be used by redeemed people as guidelines for living?"

These questions put us back between the glimpses of life and the promises of creation. They keep reminding us that education is not just for knowing. It is for doing. It means change. In this chapter it means asking the question, "How do the Ten Commandments become the ten words of life for us?"

Materials needed

Bibles • study books • chalkboard and chalk or newsprint and markers • pens or pencils • writing paper • copies of Lutheran Book of Worship *• one copy of* Prayers Based on Luther's Small Catechism *(Augsburg Fortress, 1991) • newspaper or magazine articles or photos that illustrate the Commandments • modeling clay • scissors • tape • poster board*

Before the study

___ Reflect on how you will approach your task as a teacher with the gifts and commitment. Every teacher has a style that is highly personal. The more you realize who you are, the easier it will be for you to make decisions about how to conduct the class. Personal reflection will help you imagine ways to engage class members in discussion and involve them in other activities. You will be able to teach out of your strength!

___ Think about your own reaction to the approach to the Ten Commandments taken in this course. They are not rigid answers to the questions of life but are a source out of which the questions of life are asked.

___ Get to know your class members ahead of time, if possible. Visit them in their homes or speak to them over the telephone. Make them feel welcome and appreciated.

___ Decide how you will involve the class in learning. Will you use the small groups? If so, groups of three provide a very good setting for getting maximum participation from everyone.

___ As you plan each session, imagine the whole session from beginning to end. Each part should contribute to the goals for the session.

___ Arrange for any assistance in the following area as needed: music, family night activities, worship, small group discussion leadership, and transportation.

___ Prepare the classroom or other place where the session will be held before anyone arrives. Arrange seating. Be sure the space is clean, attractive, and inviting.

 **STUDY**

ENTRY

The purpose of the activities in this section is to introduce the participants to some of the key themes of this course and the Ten Commandments with Luther's explanations from the Small Catechism.

Introductions and course overview

Take a few minutes before beginning the study for introductions. Include some comments revealing your enthusiasm for the course and commitment to what the Lutheran Faith and Life Series can offer a congregation for enrichment and growth. *Lutheran Faith and Life Planning Guide* gives a good capsule statement of the importance for studying one's heritage and the three goals for such a study (see pages 3-4).

Give a brief overview of this course as explained in "Introduction" beginning on page 4 in the study book. This will help participants know and appreciate the importance of this learning experience for their personal life and the life of the congregation. Use "Introduction" in this guide on page 3 to become familiar with the variety of ways the course can be used by itself and in conjunction with other educational programs of the congregation.

Be sure to point out other courses in the series that are being taught at the time or planned for the future in your congregation. Encourage your group to be aware of ways this adult study of Luther's Small Catechism might be linked with them, as well as with other learning programs in the congregation.

If your congregation has introduced this series with the Lutheran Heritage Event, ask those who participated in it to share what they remember about it and what the highlights were for them. Some in the class might even have helped plan that Heritage Event.

Set the tone for relationships and talk about procedures you want to follow for this course. Be clear about each person's responsibility. Tell the group what you will do and what you expect from each of them. Help participants think of themselves as both learners and teachers as they work together.

Explain that you will use small group arrangements occasionally. If the class has more than 12 members, you will probably want to use small groups frequently.

Alert class members to additional activities that may be planned for other times after some sessions, in order to be fair with time commitments you and they make to the course.

Every day life and death

Ask the participants to locate Chapter 1, "Ten Words of Life," on page 11 in the study book. You may want to ask for volunteers to read aloud the section "Every Day Life and Death" or have them read it silently to themselves.

Provide copies of daily newspapers or a selection of newspaper clippings and ask class members, either individually or in small groups, to find illustrations of the life situations in this material. Ask them to share their findings with the whole class. Use a chalkboard or newsprint to record important ideas from the discussion.

Ask the participants to comment on what these life situations mean to them. What do they think about what's going on in the world today? And why?

Help the participants realize that everyone has convictions and beliefs that determine the judgments and decisions they make. Then ask how the Ten Commandments can and do influence our beliefs and behaviors in daily life.

EXPLORING THE STUDY BOOK

Reading the Ten Commandments

The purpose of this section is to introduce the participants to the Ten Commandments by reading them along with Luther's explanations from the Small Catechism.

Ask the participants to locate Chapter 1, "Ten Words of Life," beginning on page 11 in the study book. Point out that the Ten Commandments and Luther's explanations are printed in the narrow column throughout the chapter. Have the participants quickly scan the Ten Commandments and Luther's explanations. Use the corresponding commentary, discussion questions, and Bible verses in the study book to guide the class discussion.

Key points to consider

• Be sure that the participants read the First Commandment and the commentary related to it in the study book. This Commandment is the foundation stone for the other nine Commandments as well as the whole of the Christian faith.

This Commandment is the radical announcement that God has decided to elect all people for salvation. Note that it says nothing about our claim on God. Further, God not only states his identity as "Lord" and "God" but states that all other gods are to be rejected.

• Point out that the first three Commandments concern our relationship to God. The remaining seven concern our relationship to others under the conditions of our primary relationship to God. In other words, because God is our Lord and God, this is how we will live with God and with the others whom God has elected.

• The section "What does God say of all these commandments?" (pages 19-20) is not strictly a part of the biblical Ten Commandments. Luther included this question and explanation from Exodus 20:5-6 to point to the promised result of obedience or disobedience to God.

Have the participants read this section from the Small Catechism and the corresponding commentary in the study book. Talk about the warnings and the promises claimed here.

DIGGING DEEPER

Opening comments

Begin this deeper study of this chapter by summarizing the observations under "Background" beginning on page 6 of this guide. Talk about the way the Ten Commandments can help us understand how we live every day between God's promises in creation and the heights and depths of life. Emphasize the need for studying the Ten Commandments from this point of view and for recognizing that they are not simple answers or rules for life. As a third use of the law, they can be seen as guidelines to explore with our questions and wonderings in order to discover in them God's message for today.

The study of our heritage always helps us learn something about the foundations of faith in the past that anchor and nourish us in the present. We can also see that "anchor" and "nourishment" are gifts from history. They reveal a cloud of witnesses who confessed and lived the faith long before our day.

But foundations are not enough. We must learn to build our life on them and grow into confessing, witnessing people ourselves. We cannot live just by the words and deeds of the past, as instructive as those things are. We must find our own identity in faith on the basis of the heritage we encounter and claim.

The way you lead this study will depend on whether everyone has read this chapter in the study book. Consider two approaches.

Teaching Approach A

If the chapter has not been read, your summary from this guide will be a good orientation. Then propose a general question to help participants focus their thoughts and feelings about the Commandments and get a discussion going. Ask the question, "When you think about the Ten Commandments and your life, what ideas and feelings come to mind?"

It is helpful if they can image their response. That process will encourage them to put ideas and feelings together. One way to encourage such thinking is to give each participant a piece of modeling clay and ask them to make a model of what the Ten Commandments mean in their life. They can make a model of their overall impression of the Commandments or of just one Commandment. Either way is appropriate. The choice is theirs. Give them five minutes to do this. Then put them into groups of three and give them ten minutes to tell each other what the model represents.

Call the class together. Ask each participant to write on a sheet of newsprint three to five things their experience of the Commandments tells them about God. Next, ask them to write three to five things about themselves. Put the newsprint sheets on the wall and invite them to talk with each other about their lists.

Next, ask the participants to name their favorite Commandment. Then ask them to select their least favorite Commandment. Read the Commandment and the particular commentary from the study book about it. (The commentary and Commandments are on pages 11-21 of the study book.) Invite questions. List these on the chalkboard. Point out that questions show the variety of meanings people can get out of the Commandments and that our questions help us discover what the Commandments mean for us. Now read that Commandment again along with Luther's explanation.

Divide the class into the same small groups and let them discuss the Commandments as our heritage and as a source of questions coming out of life experiences. They may wish to use the questions and Bible verses that follow each section of the commentary in the study book.

Teaching Approach B

If everyone has read this unit before the session, there are several ways you can proceed.

Option 1. Go directly to the "For Reflection" questions in Chapter 1 on pages 20-21 in the study book. The questions are broad and are not easily turned into simple answers. Divide the class into small groups and ask each group to discuss the following proposition: "Given that we have already been set free of the law through Jesus Christ and are now a new creation, how can the Ten Commandments help us live in the face of everything around us that points to death." Write this proposition on the chalkboard or newsprint for reference. Have the groups record the points of their discussion on newsprint sheets. They should work about ten minutes at this. Ask each group to report briefly to the whole class.

Option 2. Another approach is to ask each small group to take the commentary for one Commandment and formulate questions about it. Those questions will draw upon the heritage from Luther in the commentary. As time permits, discuss questions from the groups in the whole class. You might want to help the discussion with questions like, "What do the Commandments and Luther's meanings reveal about the life and death struggle Luther went through?" "Are there parallels with our struggles today?"

Option 3. Another approach is to give each person a newspaper clipping about some current event. Ask them to list several issues in the news story and how the Commandments reflect on those issues. Have them share their reflections with the whole class. Take enough time to allow each person to report briefly on at least one reflection.

Bringing it together

Whether you use teaching approach A or B, you can challenge the class with two final questions: "What is the most important thing you have come to believe about the Commandments? and "How would you live that belief and teach it to someone else?"

The value of this first encounter with heritage will be in the discussions you have been able to generate and foster in the class. This will be your biggest job and will require all your imagination and skill because you will be teaching out of the conviction that even though heritage is something we get from the past, its importance is in the way we live it.

The best way to get ready for that job is practice. Set up hypothetical situations with friends and role play. Make a list of reasons why people hesitate to discuss issues of faith and life and think of discussion-starter questions. Whenever necessary, ask "What if . . ." questions to probe or get them going.

The result will be an awareness that heritage is something that keeps growing. When we get to know it, what it means for us, and then live it, we take part in a heritage-creating experience. What we do with heritage in our lives will be the gift we give to the next generation.

FOR REFLECTION

The statements and questions under "For Reflection" on pages 20-21 in the study book are good illustrations of the relationship between what we believe and questions about daily life that grow out of them. Each statement begins with a declaration followed by a question.

It seems natural to begin with the questions. Some class members, however, might want to start with the declarations and use them for discussion. If limited class time will not permit using all of the questions, select one or two, or allow small groups to select questions that interest them. Focus on these questions.

OUR PRAYERS

Close the session with the devotion suggested in this section on page 21 of the study book. If you used clay models, select one or two as a focus piece. You can introduce or surround the whole experience with a stanza from a Reformation hymn such as "God's Word Is Our Great Heritage" (*LBW* 239). You might also use a commandment prayer from *Prayers Based on Luther's Small Catechism*.

✝ POST-STUDY

Expanding the learning

☐ As a class, find other places or classes in your congregation where the Small Catechism touches other people in their journeys in faith. For example, youth in confirmation classes, parents and sponsors of a child about to be baptized or confirmed, a recent adult Baptism, congregational committees discussing social concerns, a friend who wants to learn more about the Lutheran expression of faith.

☐ Invite a lawyer, judge, or police officer to your class to talk about the function of law to bring about order and protection to a community.

☐ Make a banner or poster that communicates the blessing and promises of keeping the Ten Commandments.

☐ Depending on the size of the class, divide into two teams to play charades. Use the Commandments as the items to be acted out. The members of the other group are to guess which Commandment is being acted.

Looking ahead

• If you decide to spend more than one session on this chapter, make clear what will be covered in the next class meeting. Assign any reading from the study book or Bible to help the participants prepare for the next session.

• Read through the parts of the study book and this guide that will be the focus of the next session.

• Decide how you will use the Small Catechism and commentary in the study book.

• Work through the questions in the commentary and under "For Reflection" and plan which ones you will use.

• Decide which of the "Expanding the Learning" activities you will use or encourage the participants to use.

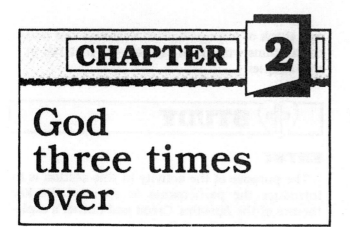

CHAPTER 2

God three times over

FOCUS STATEMENT

God is the one who created all things and continues to create. God is the one working in creation to restore it and to establish peace and harmony. God is the one who is present now as Father, Son, and Holy Spirit to bring you and all creation to its fullness in the age to come.

OBJECTIVES

This chapter will help adults:
- learn about the Apostles' Creed as a witness to Scripture;
- develop a way for looking and listening for faith in God within the church;
- live their faith in the world.

PRE-STUDY

Background: The Apostles' Creed

Faith in God is never just a personal or individual experience, even though it is within ourselves that we know and confess it. It comes to us through the community of the faithful witnesses who have heard God's word in Scripture, seen it in life, and put it into a statement of faith we know as the Apostles' Creed.

The Apostles' Creed is an early Christian understanding of God revealed through Scripture. It was the early church's confession of God by which they ordered their lives in the community of faith and in the world. Though this Creed is not long, it makes clear that for those Christians who lived in the light of Jesus' resurrection, God was no simple matter, limited to what individuals perceive and understand.

Scripture reveals a God who is closely involved in our lives and in everything that is part of the world we know. God created the universe from nothing. God promised to be present with us and for us to help us make sense out of history.

God is for us in times of joy and also in times of great suffering and even death. God is all this and more.

When the early Christians listened to what Scripture said, they had to speak about God in three ways. First, God is the one who created all things and who continues to create. The image in this awareness of God is the parent. Second, God is the one working in creation to restore it and to establish peace and harmony. The image in this awareness of God is the redeemer. Third, God is the one who is present now in creation with caring compassion to bring creation to its fullness in the age to come. The image in this awareness of God is the life-giving spirit of God. Father, Son, and Holy Spirit, God three times over, creating, redeeming, and bringing all things to wholeness.

What does one do in the presence of such a God? The early Christians wrote a creed. But their doing that was more than what we normally think of as putting beliefs into a statement of faith. When the early Christians said, "I believe in Father, Son, and Holy Spirit," they set their hearts on God and opened their lives to the overwhelming reality of God's presence with them.

Luther's explanations of the three articles or parts of the Apostles' Creed continue the long line of tradition of making sense out of God's revealed word for life. This process is never one that proves or disproves God. It is a process that helps people come to understand the gracious decision God has made in Christ to save us without any merit on our part. With such grace given, we respond in a confession of faith.

This means we cannot neatly separate what we call "facts" from "beliefs" either about creation or Jesus or the age to come. We believe in order to understand, and we understand in order to believe, as Anselm said (A.D. 1033-1109).

As God's Word given for life, Scripture and the Apostles' Creed call us to faith individually and communally. In so doing, they proclaim to us some answers for questions about God and the world. But they also present new questions as we think and wonder about life under God. It is through these answers and questions that we hear what God has to say to us.

Luther's explanation of each article in the Apostles' Creed helps us toward that end. The First Article affirms what Scripture says about God's creating work and our place in it. God not only brought everything into existence, but God also continues to sustain it.

The Second Article makes it clear that we are ultimately dependent on the grace of God shown in the life, death, and resurrection of Jesus

Christ. Neither our thinking about God nor creation can set us free; Christ does!

In the Third Article we are told that the grace of God comes through the Holy Spirit. Even faith is not our doing, but it is the work of the Spirit. God works faith in us, setting us free from sin, death, and the devil. The Spirit then gathers us into the community of the faithful—the holy Christian church.

Materials needed

Bibles • study books • chalkboard and chalk or newsprint and markers • pens or pencils • writing paper • copies of Lutheran Book of Worship *• one copy of* Prayers Based on Luther's Small Catechism *(Augsburg Fortress, 1991) • worship books from other denominations (optional) • books about other faith traditions (optional)*

Before the study

Your attitude about believing as involving both the content of what is believed and a disposition of the mind and heart will be an important model for the objectives of this session and a witness to the way creeds function in the community of faith. Take some time to reflect on this matter after you have read the study book and the materials in this guide. Have a position in your own mind about this and be ready to help the class members come to a position of their own.

In a similar way, the matter of living with questions as well as with answers will be something for you to think about in terms of discussion in the class. Think of ways to illustrate how the questions we have about life lead to further growth and understanding. Be ready to apply this approach to what the Apostles' Creed says.

___ Think about the activity "How Much Can I Change" on pages 13-14 of this guide and have the steps clearly in mind.

___ If you plan to discuss varieties of religious beliefs, become acquainted with other religious denominations through encyclopedia articles or books you can find in the public or church libraries.

___ The study book refers to Robert Bellah's book, *Habits of the Heart* (Harper & Row, 1985). If possible, read Chapter 9, "Religion," pages 219-249.

___ Make inquiries in the congregation about other Lutheran Faith and Life Series programs

and think of ways your class members can make connections with them through the material in this chapter.

 # STUDY

ENTRY

The purpose of the activity in this section is to introduce the participants to some of the key themes of the Apostles' Creed and Luther's explanation from the Small Catechism.

Use this section of this guide and the study book to highlight the following thoughts about creeds and their functions. Together, the materials provide an opportunity for participants to begin talking about their own beliefs, what they have discovered about the beliefs of others, and how all that relates to the Apostles' Creed as part of the worship experience in the Sunday liturgy.

Not long ago

Ask the participants to locate the section "Not Long Ago" on page 23 in their study books. You may want to ask for a volunteer or two to read aloud this section or have the participants quickly scan it for themselves. Share some or all of the following comments with the participants.

Religiously, we are living in a time of great variety. This variety can be seen both close at home, in our immediate communities and friends, and throughout the world among other religions. We know many things today about what other people believe.

For people who have any faith commitment at all, such knowledge leads to questions such as, "What does this variety mean?" and "How does one live with it?"

The challenge of variety can be enriching. What other people believe, even the differences we find within the Christian community, can be a stimulus to think further about the way we understand and live the claims of faith expressed in the church's creeds.

An illusion we often live by is that all Christians believe the same things, especially the fundamentals of the faith. It is easy to come to that conclusion when we give attention to such things as creeds. Creeds put the content of faith into words.

As statements of faith, creeds help us to be more and more conscious of what and why we believe. They help us live among many claims about truth and a variety of beliefs without losing our own commitment.

The Apostles' Creed serves two functions. It provides the beliefs of the church we can learn in order to live the faith. It also provides the setting in which we can live the faith in order to learn it.

EXPLORING THE STUDY BOOK

Reading the Apostles' Creed

The purpose of this section is to introduce the participants to the Apostles' Creed by reading it along with Luther's explanations from the Small Catechism.

Ask the participants to locate Chapter 2, "God Three Times Over," beginning on page 23 in the study book. Point out that the Apostles' Creed and Luther's explanations are printed in the narrow column throughout the chapter. Have the participants quickly scan the Apostles' Creed and Luther's explanations. Use them and the corresponding commentary, discussion questions, and Bible verses in the study book to guide the discussion.

Key points to consider

• In discussing the First Article, point out how Luther moves quickly from "God in general" to "God in particular"—"God has created *me* . . . He has given *me*" (emphasis added).

• Notice how God is concerned with our whole being and not our disembodied "souls." In Luther's original German, part of the meaning of this article can be translated: "my body and soul, eyes, and ears, and all my members, my reason and all my senses were given and are still preserved" by God.

• In the Second Article, note how again Luther moves from general history to particular salvation—"At great cost he [Jesus Christ] has saved and redeemed *me*. . . ." Luther was not here concerned with the historical events of Jesus' life but with what his death does to us and for us.

• In the Third Article, point out that the Holy Spirit was given to create the faith in us that God demands. See Article V of The Augsburg Confession in the *Book of Concord*, page 31 (Fortress Press, 1959).

• Talk about how the Holy Spirit works through God's Word, the church, and other people to bring salvation.

DIGGING DEEPER

Opening comments

When discussing faith, it is important to begin the learning process where people are in their levels of understanding and faith development. Learning about the Apostles' Creed is more than just learning what Luther said it meant. One can learn the words of a creed in school, but to learn the faith one needs to find it being lived in the believing community. Before examining Luther's explanations of the articles of the Apostles' Creed, help the participants gain a sense of what "commitment" means to them.

For most people, believing is a highly personal matter, even when believing has to do with the community's faith. Therefore, Sheila's faith as described in *Habits of the Heart*, page 221 (Harper & Row, 1985), is a good place to begin a discussion of faith that will be centered in a creed.

Divide the class into groups of two or three and ask each group to discuss Sheila's faith and what the study book says about it on page 23. Encourage participants to talk about how much they identify with Sheila's understanding of what faith is, apart from her actual belief. After about five minutes, bring the class back together. Ask for volunteers to briefly share their conversations from small groups. In this way, you may help class members identify their feelings about belief as well as their understanding of the things people actually believe.

Statements of Faith

Invite each person to write a brief comment answering the statement: "How I came to be a person of faith." Ask them to identify how people, events, and other experiences have significantly shaped their lives as Christians. Have them identify people they have looked up to as models for the Christian life.

Then ask individuals to share what they have written. Make a list of things they mention on the chalkboard or newsprint. Let the group examine the list and note things that are common and different. Have the class draw conclusions from this list about the significance of relationships in the community of faith.

How much can I change?

Use the following steps:

1. Ask each person to write down on a sheet of paper or tell another person what is most important for them about the Christian faith.

2. Have them discuss in pairs what they have written or said with one other person.

3. Call the class together and ask members to take the place of the other person, accepting what the other person said is most important about the Christian faith as one's own.

4. Ask each person to share with a different person how life would be changed if it were seriously influenced by the faith of the other person.

Bringing it together

At this point you have helped the participants identify their thoughts and feelings about the faith for themselves and others. Now you can take up the commentary in the study book on Luther's explanations of the three articles of the Apostles' Creed.

Introduce the notion of the interdependence of the articles of the Apostles' Creed under the image used in the title, "God Three Times Over." Select one article and discuss what has been said in the commentary in the study book. If you prefer, let the class make the selection of the article to be discussed.

As the discussion progresses, use the chalkboard or newsprint to make a list of answers and a list of questions that the article of the Creed suggests. Let these lists be the focus for a discussion on the importance of finding answers and generating questions.

Point out that answers we find in the Apostles' Creed for our journey in faith are always just starting points. They give us an orientation and start us going in a particular direction. As we move forward in the journey, we meet others traveling the same way and find encouragement and enrichment.

Along with encouragement and enrichment, we find new questions that keep us open to growth. Questions about faith help us grow in faith.

FOR REFLECTION

The first question under "For Reflection" on page 32 in the study book might generate more questions before a discussion can be fruitful. For example, the phrase "the nature and work of the three 'persons' of the Trinity" might evoke questions about how we can speak of the "threeness" of God. In dealing with such a situation, it is best not to use concrete picture examples, such as a triangle or three interlocking rings. Instead, use the image of "God Three Times Over" in the study book and "Background" beginning on page 11 in this guide.

Question 2 provides a good opportunity to talk about our responsibility in the face of all God does for us.

Question 3 has to do with the way we are made one with God through Jesus' death. We call this the atonement. There are different ideas about that in Scripture.

Question 4 can be used as a basis for discussing the Third Article of the Apostles' Creed anywhere in the session.

OUR PRAYERS

Begin with the hymn, "Faith of Our Fathers" (*LBW* 500). You may or may not substitute the word *parents* for *fathers*. Then follow the suggestions under "Our Prayers" on page 32 in the study book. Select a prayer from *Prayers Based on Luther's Small Catechism* for the closing prayer.

 **POST-STUDY**

Expanding the session

☐ Ask class members to talk with confirmation teachers to discuss ways for connecting the experience in this session with the study of the Apostles' Creed there.

☐ Ask two or three farmers to come to class and discuss why they plant seeds, what is expected, and what happens if the crop is lost. Why do they continue farming, given the risks of failure?

☐ Have each participant interview two or three people and ask them what it is they know about Jesus Christ. Compare the lists.

☐ Invite a Native North American who follows his or her tribal religion to talk with the class about his or her religion. Compare the comments with the Christian concepts of God and the Holy Spirit.

☐ Ask a long-term member of your congregation to speak with the class about the history of your congregation—its ministry and the people who formed the congregation.

Looking ahead

• If you decide to spend more than one session on this chapter, make clear what will be covered in the next class meeting. Assign any reading from the study book or Bible to help the participants prepare for the next session.

• Read through the parts of the study book and this guide that will be the focus of the next session.

• Decide how you will use the Small Catechism and commentary in the study book.

• Work through the questions in the commentary and under "For Reflection" and plan which ones you will use.

• Decide which of the "Expanding the Learning" activities you will use or encourage the participants to use.

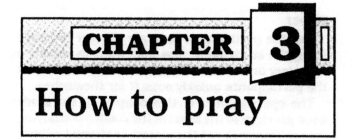

CHAPTER 3

How to pray

FOCUS STATEMENT

Prayer always involves what we think about God and the relationship we can have with God. These thoughts can produce a cozy feeling or a strenuous encounter that seems to place one at risk.

OBJECTIVES

This chapter will help adults:

- understand the meaning of the Lord's Prayer and its place in the life of the believer;
- be open to the relationship with God that prayer brings about;
- grow in a personal prayer life.

 **PRE-STUDY**

Background: The Lord's Prayer

Prayer is a perennial experience. It never goes away. It keeps us asking questions about why we pray and how and what we say in our conversations with God.

Such experience prompted the disciples' request, "Lord, teach us to pray" (Luke 11:1). Jesus responded with a prayer we know as the Lord's Prayer. It stands at the center of everything Christians have said and done about prayer in the history of Christianity. It is at the center of our communion and conversation with God, too.

This means that prayer has many expressions, depending on one's relationship with God. Prayer follows the pattern of other kinds of conversation and communion. Sometimes we speak boldly with great understanding or frustration and anguish. Sometimes conversation is timid and halting because of uncertainty or anxiety. Sometimes what we want to say is clear as we say it. At other times, words don't seem to be available to convey what is in our mind and heart. So with prayer.

Such variety, however, is not self-defeating. Prayer doesn't lose its power or significance because it comes to expression in so many ways. Rather, this variety points to the continuing human need to pray without ceasing in whatever way one can through whatever life brings.

Even though prayer is rooted in the inner life, it is part of one's growth in the community of faith. But it is not something that happens automatically or even naturally. The disciples were together when they came to Jesus and asked him to teach them to pray. Jesus taught them a prayer that was filled with the tradition and heritage of the community of faith and involved the whole person. As such, it is a prayer for us, his contemporary disciples.

The image of prayer as conversation or communion means that both partners are involved in listening and speaking. In prayer, we become open to ways God can affect us and we can let God know our concerns. That is both the risk and the promise of prayer. It is risky to open oneself to the mutuality in any conversation. In prayer, the risk is ultimate; but so is the hope. If we risk human conversations in the hope of all they can produce, when we risk conversation with God in prayer we do so in the hope of God's promise to hear our prayer in love and compassion.

There is no guarantee about what the conversation with God in prayer will produce. The promise that God will hear our prayer in love and compassion is all that is guaranteed. The good of prayer is not dependent on the outcome of prayer. Something is given in the act of praying itself beyond all we say or do. This means that the answer to prayer may be in terms other than the concrete requests of prayer. What we sometimes offer to God to be changed may be the very things through which the strength of God is revealed. God's answer to Paul, "My grace is sufficient for you, for power is made perfect in weakness" (2 Corinthians 12:9), is the reminder that the outcome of conversation with God is not always joyful deliverance but a call to obedience for God's sake.

When we learn to pray, we learn something about ourselves and God. In the Lord's Prayer that learning is very specific and particular by the way this prayer determines how we are to pray. It begins with God as a loving caregiver whose grace toward us is abundant beyond measure.

Jesus taught his disciples that such graciousness is the start of prayer, allowing God's presence to set the agenda. Only then do our needs in the petitions that follow become part of a real conversation rather than a list of wants. Jesus said that when we pray we must remember that God is listening. The effect of that remembering is that we can talk about our needs with God in mind.

Someone has said that the Lord's Prayer lives life backward, from a tomorrow that is sure to the uncertainties of today. It begins with "Your kingdom come." If we can pray that petition with any real enthusiasm, then the petitions for our daily needs that follow are more than enough.

Materials needed

Bibles • study books • chalkboard and chalk or newsprint and markers • pens or pencils • writing paper • copies of Lutheran Book of Worship *• one copy of* Prayers Based on Luther's Small Catechism *• books on Christian prayer • several daily newspapers • "Listening in on the Lord's Prayer" worksheets (see "Before the Study" below)*

Before the study

___ Refresh your memory on experiences of prayer in your life.

___ Think about the claim the Lord's Prayer has in your life. How would you talk about that to a friend or a stranger? Does the following sentence from the study book fit your experience: "It (the Lord's Prayer) is safe enough to wade in and deep enough to swim in at the same time" (page 33)?

___ Obtain some resource books on prayer from the church and public libraries.

___ Prepare "Listening in on the Lord's Prayer" worksheet. Photocopy one for each member of the class. Put the title at the top of a sheet of typing paper with the following questions spaced equally down the page: **1.** *What assumptions does the Lord's Prayer make about God and the one who prays the prayer?* **2.** *Are there some unspoken implications about our relationship with God in the Lord's Prayer under the surface of the words?* **3.** *What images about one's relationship with God does the Lord's Prayer bring to mind?*

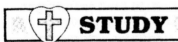 **STUDY**

ENTRY

The purpose of the activities in this section is to introduce the participants to some of the key themes of the Lord's Prayer and Luther's explanations from the Small Catechism.

Prayer

Ask the participants to locate "Prayer" on page 33 in the study book. You may want to ask for a volunteer or two to read aloud this section or have the participants quickly scan it for themselves.

The opening lines of this chapter in the study book get right to the heart of the matter of studying prayer. Prayer is not the easiest or clearest subject for involving people in discussion. People are often hesitant to talk about prayer in any public place, even within a church study group. There are probably many reasons for this. But under them all is the nature of prayer as being highly personal and even private in the minds of many people. Therefore, as you enter the subject of prayer with your group, it is important to begin with a recognition of this hesitancy and be sensitive to where people are in their readiness to discuss prayer.

The experience of prayer

Sensitivity helps one develop and use a positive, encouraging attitude with learners. Let people identify and claim their experiences in prayer, whatever those experiences have been. Ask them to describe experiences of prayer when they were children or adolescents or since they entered the world of adulthood. By starting with their early years, you allow them to distance themselves from practices they might have since changed, practices about which they can talk more objectively. Be accepting of what they say and avoid words or attitudes that communicate negative judgments.

Most important is how the Lord's Prayer is held up to people. As people talk about their experiences, be alert for attitudes they have about the Lord's Prayer. Help them to understand that the Lord's Prayer is not the only prayer to use or the divine substitute for all our efforts to talk with God. Lead them to an appreciation of this prayer as Jesus' model for prayer offered first to the disciples to help them pray their own prayers.

Other ways prayer can be expressed besides words include dance and movement. Every form of expression communicates something a little different from others and yields a different experience. So in prayer, when we pray with expressions other than words, we communicate something different from what we can through words. In this way, different forms of prayer can be mutually enriching.

After you have explored these assumptions and the ideas people bring with them to a study of prayer, turn to the questions "What is prayer?" and "Why pray?" in the commentary text on page 34 of the study book. These questions are raised and discussed in terms of Luther's explanation of the Lord's Prayer. They will help you and the class focus directly upon the material in the Small Catechism.

EXPLORING THE STUDY BOOK

Reading the Lord's Prayer

The purpose of this section is to introduce the participants to the petitions of the Lord's Prayer by reading them along with Luther's explanations from the Small Catechism.

Ask the participants to locate Chapter 3, "How to Pray," beginning on page 33 in the study book. Point out that the Lord's Prayer and Luther's explanations are printed in the narrow column throughout the chapter. Have the participants quickly scan the petitions of the Lord's Prayer and Luther's explanations. Use the corresponding commentary, discussion questions and Bible verses in the study book to guide the class discussion.

Key points to consider

• Point out that God as Father is not based on creation, but upon God's redeeming and saving us "from sin, death, and the power of the devil." See the discussion of God as Father in Chapter 2 of the study book on pages 26-27.

• Discuss Nichol's statement that the introduction and first three petitions "are not so much about God's name, message, rule, or even God's will, as they are about us" (pages 34-35 of the study book).

• Point out that the Fourth Petition echoes Luther's meaning of the First Article of the Apostles' Creed.

• The Fifth, Sixth, and Seventh Petitions deal with the intersection of our relationship with God and our relationship with others.

• In the Fifth Petition, point out that our forgiveness by God is not dependent upon our forgiving of others. As Nichol wrote, "God's forgiveness makes possible and is represented in your forgiveness of others" (page 37 of the study book).

DIGGING DEEPER

Opening comments

The suggestions under "Entry" beginning on page 16 of this guide and "Prayer" beginning on page 33 in the study book offer a broad base for a discussion of prayer. This is intentional in order that class members might first be encouraged to talk about prayer as they have experienced it and then develop a dialog of questions and wonderings about prayer in terms of Luther's explanations for the Lord's Prayer.

This format will require some adjustments in the time spent on both the entry materials and the study of the Lord's Prayer itself. Perhaps it will be best to devote equal amounts of time to each.

Listening three ways

As you take up the petitions in the Lord's Prayer, explain that the approach will be to listen. Prayer is conversation with God, and the Lord's Prayer is Jesus' suggestion to the disciples about what that conversation should be like. The primary task in this session will be "to listen in" on that conversation.

Explain that the class will listen in at three levels: listening to the prayer itself, listening to what Luther heard when he listened, and listening to the commentary in the study book. These levels of listening will draw us deeper into the prayer and its meaning for our life and will enrich our personal prayer life, in whatever form we express it.

In the Lord's Prayer, Jesus told his disciples something about who they were as children of God. So with us. The more attention we give to that prayer, following its meaning through the many facets of conversation it evokes, the more we will know about ourselves as children of God.

For the first level, divide the class into groups of two and ask each group to put into their own words what they hear in this prayer-conversation. Distribute the worksheet "Listening in on the Lord's Prayer" and copies of *Lutheran Book of Worship*. Point out that two versions of the Lord's Prayer appear on page 71. Have the groups use the questions on the worksheet as a guide as they listen in.

Point out that just as in any conversation the listener needs to figure out what the words are really saying, so in prayer. For example, as we use and listen to the Lord's Prayer, what is going on in that conversation? What kind of conversation did Jesus suggest in this model prayer? What do we hear ourselves saying, and what does the prayer imply about God's part in this conversation?

Then call everyone back together and have the groups report. List things they say on the chalkboard or newsprint.

In the second level of listening we concentrate on what Luther said about the Lord's Prayer. Ask class members to identify a petition that is meaningful to them and to briefly explain why. On the chalkboard or newsprint, list the petitions in one column and the reasons in a parallel column.

Now ask everyone to think about what Luther said concerning the favorite petition, noting similarities and differences between their reasons and Luther's explanations printed in the study book.

After they have had some time to reflect, refer back to the chalkboard and ask for volunteers to share their reflections on similarities and differences in respect to Luther's explanations.

The third level of listening is the contemporary level where we have an opportunity to listen to each other. We do this listening in three ways.

First, we listen to a contemporary voice commenting on Luther. Second, we listen to each other discuss what that commentary says. Third, we make an assessment about how well both Luther and the commentary intersect our own experiences of prayer.

Divide the class into groups of three. Ask each group to read and talk about the comments made in the study book about the Third Petition, the Seventh Petition, and the Doxology (see pages 35, 38 of the study book). After the discussion, give each group part of a newspaper and ask the group to select a slice of daily life from it—a news report or interest story—and discuss how the Lord's Prayer applies. Some petitions will be more relevant than others.

Bring the groups together and have a general discussion of the conclusions from each. This might stimulate thoughts about how the Lord's Prayer intersects the personal life situation of class members. Encourage a discussion of this thought. It will give a focus for the last two suggestions for approaching this session.

The first is to help class members assess their own attitudes and feelings about prayer and to think about the use of prayer in their lives. Indicate that developing one's prayer life has to be intentional. It does not happen automatically or naturally. Also point out that the best way to do this is with the support and encouragement of the community of faith. This means not only finding support for one's self but also giving support to others.

Finally, ask the whole class, "How do you pray best?" As class members talk about favorite prayers, gestures, times, and occasions, point out that this sharing can be the beginning of finding support and giving support for a life of prayer that is centered on all that the prayer of Jesus means.

FOR REFLECTION

If the discussions throughout the session raised questions that could not be pursued at the time, return to them now.

This might be a time to review what was said in the session on the Apostles' Creed about the importance of questions in the life of faith. People usually have many questions when it comes to prayer. Now is a good time to affirm and encourage these questions for discussion in the community of faith.

Specifically, the questions under "For Reflection" on page 39 in the study book build upon the session activities. Question 1 pursues what was discussed about prayer as conversation and the suggestions

about different forms of prayer. Question 2 is a challenge to affirm the reality of God's kingdom in life but not to identify life with that kingdom. The activity about applying the Lord's Prayer to what we find in the daily newspaper can be grist for the third question. Question 4 leads back to the material in "Background" beginning on page 15.

OUR PRAYERS

If there is someone in the class or congregation who can offer a prayer in dance movements, invite that person to begin the devotion time. Otherwise, start with the hymn, "Christians, While on Earth Abiding" (*LBW* 440). Then follow the meditation suggestions in the study book and close with the hymn, "Praise God from Whom All Blessings Flow" (*LBW* 565). You may also want to select a prayer from the section on the Lord's Prayer in *Prayers Based on Luther's Small Catechism*.

 **POST-STUDY**

Expanding the session

☐ Display books of prayer and encourage the class members to browse. Invite them to do follow-up reading either in books about prayer or in books of prayer. Send them to the church or public library to find what they can on the subject of prayer.

☐ Encourage participants to join neighborhood prayer groups or prayer breakfasts if these are available in your community or church.

☐ Talk to your pastor about a retreat for prayer and spiritual growth that could be held on a weekend or at another convenient time.

☐ Encourage attention to prayer in home settings.

Looking ahead

• If you decide to spend more than one session on this chapter, make clear what will be covered in the next class meeting. Assign any reading from the study book or Bible to help the participants prepare for the next session.

• Read through the parts of the study book and this guide that will be the focus of the next session.

• Decide how you will use the Small Catechism and commentary in the study book.

• Work through the questions in the commentary and under "For Reflection" and plan which ones you will use.

• Decide which of the "Expanding the Learning" activities you will use or encourage the participants to use.

CHAPTER 4

From death to life

FOCUS STATEMENT

The gift of Baptism is life now and forever. God gives us life by setting us free through the forgiveness of sin. In that gift is the promise of God's presence from day to day and in the life to come.

OBJECTIVES

This chapter will help adults:
- learn about Baptism as God's promise of life;
- appreciate their own Baptism and their part in the baptized life of others in the community of faith;
- continue to grow and live in the awareness of their Baptism.

 **PRE-STUDY**

Background: Holy Baptism

The gospel is God's promise of life and the forgiveness of sins. The words of the gospel bear that promise to us and secure it as the words themselves take hold of our lives when we hear them and believe them. Words have the power to transform.

There is a childhood saying: "Sticks and stones may break my bones, but words can never hurt me." It is a saying children use to defend themselves from name-calling. But we all know that such a defense is a weak one because name-calling can hurt just as much as physical blows.

Words have power, but not just to hurt. They can also heal and restore life. A word of forgiveness is one such word. It can turn around the hurt and put a broken relationship back together again.

In our life together, words are enough to convey the message of hurt and healing. And if this is so in our human discourse, how much more sure can we be when the promise made is God's Word!

In the hearing of the gospel, God gives life and the forgiveness of sins. Jesus bound God's Word to earthly realities in water, bread, and wine so that we could not miss that life-giving Word and for us to experience them again and again.

Baptism was given so that we can have life as God's children. We know it visibly in water that is both a part of our home in the world and a symbol of God's creating act. Baptism is a drowning of our old sinful selves. It is a washing or cleansing for new life. Baptism is the word of God connected with the water but not the water alone. As a visible word, water provides an important way for us to interpret and understand Baptism.

Through our Baptism, God fully forgives our sins. Then God places us into a community where the life of faith is lived and known. We are adopted into that experience. It is not our birthright or a claim we can make on the basis of our achievements or merit. It does not depend on our own worth or our understanding. It is pure gift, God's doing.

Baptism is always a communal experience. Though it happens to individuals, it happens within a community and affects everyone in it. Just as every human community is changed when a new member arrives, so the community of faith is changed whenever someone enters it through Baptism.

When someone is baptized, we need to make a place for the baptized person to grow in faith. We need to allow for new relationships to emerge among believers and for a new community to be formed. When the liturgy of Holy Baptism is over, the whole community needs to establish itself all over again. That is why the baptismal liturgy ends appropriately with the exchange of peace. The ministers, the baptized, sponsors, parents, and the congregation offer the word of peace to each other as they walk together into a new life.

The gift of Baptism is life now and forever. God gives us life by setting us free through the forgiveness of sin. In that gift is the promise of God's presence from day to day and in the life to come.

Baptism reminds us what Scripture says, that we are called and enabled to live in daily newness of life (Romans 6:4). It also reminds us that this life leads beyond itself. This age will come to an end (Matthew 28:20), and beyond it is the fullness of God's reign to which we shall be heirs. In Baptism, God frees us "from sin, death, and the power of the devil." Because we are God's baptized we can live in this world for the sake of others.

Baptism provides encouragement and strength. It is a mark upon us, the sign of Christ by which we are reminded of God's continued help in spite of our failings and the problems, hurts, and troubles of life.

In those times in Luther's life when everything seemed to turn against him, the anchor that firmly grounded his hope was Baptism. He clung with confidence to the promise of God in his Baptism. In spite of all else, he could say, "I have been baptized." And so can we.

Baptism draws us close to God and enlivens our trust in God. In its act of washing by water, we are placed at the gracious mercy of God to receive God's transforming word that gives life. Lest we make God a servant of that gracious act, we must remember that Baptism is always the actual Word of God. Through Baptism we are made right with God because of God's Word and the faith the Holy Spirit creates in us that comes from that Word.

Baptism is an experience of dying to the old and being raised to new life. There are many images for such a transforming experience. The one the apostle Paul chose was that of the death and resurrection of Jesus. The act of Baptism is that dramatic and consuming. It is nothing less than the death, burial, and resurrection of Jesus.

The life of the baptized takes place in the community of faith in the world. It is not a life that just happens willy-nilly. The life promised in Baptism is a gift to grasp every day of our life. It is a gift of growing up in faith, of living it and practicing it. Baptism is the beginning of a journey in faith that is led by the Holy Spirit and accompanied by a community of believers.

Materials needed

Bibles • study books • chalkboard and chalk or newsprint and markers • pens or pencils • writing paper • copies of Lutheran Book of Worship *• one copy of* Prayers Based on Luther's Small Catechism *• "My Life and Baptism" worksheets (see "Before the Study" below) • one copy of* Occasional Services: A Companion to Lutheran Book of Worship (1982).

Before the study

__ Recall as much information as you can about your own Baptism and its significance for your daily life and work. This will help you appreciate the ideas and activities for the class members.

__ Prepare the worksheet "My Life and Baptism." Put that title at the top of a sheet of typing paper and space the following questions on the page: **1.** *What does the liturgy tell me about my life with God and in the world?* **2.** *What are the struggles I have living this liturgy?* **3.** *How can*

this liturgy help me live into my Baptism? Make one copy for each participant.

__ Locate a copy of *Occasional Services: A Companion to Lutheran Book of Worship.* Ask your pastor if she or he has a copy.

__ Think about how you might use Questions 2 and 3 under "For Reflection" (on page 47 of the study book) during the session.

 **STUDY**

ENTRY

The purpose of the activities in this section is to introduce the participants to some of the key themes of the sacraments (especially the Sacrament of Holy Baptism) and Luther's explanations from the Small Catechism.

The Bible teaches

Ask the participants to locate "The Bible Teaches" on page 41 in their study books. You may want to ask for a volunteer or two to read aloud this section or have the participants quickly scan it for themselves.

The entry materials provide an opportunity to introduce both sacraments, Baptism and the Lord's Supper, as the means of grace and to focus upon the subject of Baptism in this session.

These sacraments come to us out of the life and ministry of Jesus. Both are commanded by him and carry the promise of God's blessing. Both are connected with visible, earthly elements. As such, Baptism and the Lord's Supper are vehicles or means of grace. Through the sacraments, God comes to us to proclaim and to make actual God's continuing, unconditional love for us.

Tell the participants that the word *sacraments* comes from the Latin word meaning "an oath of allegiance and a promise of fidelity." Soldiers, for example, would bind themselves to their leaders through a *sacramentum.*

Promises and pledges

After introducing the two sacraments (Baptism and the Lord's Supper) and speaking about the meaning of the word *sacrament,* distribute paper and have each member of the class make a list of promises and pledges made to other people. Ask them to divide the sheet into three columns. Have them title the left-hand column "People in the promises and pledges." Title the middle column "Promises and pledges I gave" and title the right-hand column "Promises and pledges I received."

Divide the class into groups of three and ask each person to share with the others what they put on the sheet. Tell them to talk about what was involved in the relationships they had with others over promises and pledges. For example, ask if the strength of the relationship was in the word of promise or in something tangible.

Have a general discussion about the importance of trust and belief in our understanding and use of sacraments. This discussion can follow naturally on what the class has just done to emphasize God's promise and can provide the background for a study of the commentary in the study book.

EXPLORING THE STUDY BOOK

Reading the Sacrament of Holy Baptism

The purpose of this section is to introduce the participants to the Sacrament of Holy Baptism by reading it along with Luther's explanations in the Small Catechism.

Ask the participants to locate Chapter 4, "From Death to Life," beginning on page 41 in the study book. Point out that the Sacrament of Holy Baptism and Luther's explanations are printed in the narrow column throughout the chapter. Have the participants quickly scan the Sacrament of Holy Baptism and Luther's explanations. Use the corresponding commentary, discussion questions, and Bible verses in the study book to guide the class discussion.

Key points to consider

• Under the question "What is Baptism?" in the Small Catechism, help the participants see the primacy of God's Word and command given with and in the water.

• Talk about the importance of water for life. Ask why Jesus (and other religions) chose water as a sign of new life.

• Discuss how infant Baptism, as practiced by Lutherans and other Christians, shows that God is the one who is active in Baptism and not the human will.

• Many adults may think of their Baptism as being a past event. Discuss together how Luther's explanations help to make Baptism a present and daily event.

DIGGING DEEPER

"My Life and Baptism" worksheet

One of the best ways to help people understand the communal aspects of the Sacrament of Holy Baptism and the individual's experience of it is to have them read the service for Holy Baptism in a worship book.

Give each person a copy of *Lutheran Book of Worship* and ask them to turn to the liturgy for Holy Baptism beginning on page 121. (If your congregation uses another order of service for Holy Baptism, provide copies of that order.) Distribute the worksheets "My Life and Baptism" and give time for each to read the liturgy and reflect on the questions. Then divide the class into groups of three and ask them to share their reflections from the worksheets.

This experience can raise personal awareness of Baptism and lead into a general discussion about individual experiences of this sacrament. If any in the class were baptized as young people or adults, ask them to share their memories. You may want to invite class members to tell what they experience of Baptism whenever a Baptism occurs in church. Lead this discussion to the topic of Baptism in one's daily life, picking up on the reflections on the worksheets.

Other questions might arise from the worksheets and general discussion. You may wish to discuss different methods of Baptism—total immersion, sprinkling, pouring, or believer Baptism. Concentrate your discussion on the experiences of Baptism in daily life. Keep a chalkboard or newsprint sheet to record other ideas and questions for later consideration as time permits.

Living your Baptism

You can develop the theme about Baptism in daily life by encouraging class members to think about the idea of living their own Baptism. Start by asking how many remember their baptismal date. Ask if any celebrate the anniversary of their Baptism or that of a friend or family member. Illustrate possibilities for remembering and celebrating the anniversary by acquainting the class with the service for an "Anniversary of a Baptism" in *Occasional Services* (pages 23-26). Your pastor may have a copy of this book. The suggestions in this service can be used in the intimate setting of the home, with close friends, or at a special service in church.

In addition to a liturgical ritual for observing baptismal anniversaries, individuals should be encouraged to talk more about Baptism to others in the church, send greeting cards to those having an anniversary, and support baptismal sponsors in fulfilling their promises at the time of Baptism.

Baptismal sponsors

Ask the class how many have been or will be sponsors at a Baptism, and how many remember or maintain contact with their sponsors. Such contact is often impossible, given mobility and age. But sponsorship continues to be an important way to encourage supportive connections within the community of faith as we live into our Baptism. This is a topic that could be discussed generally and might lead to suggestions on ways to have surrogate sponsors in one's present congregation.

Sponsors and parents serve similar functions in the Sacrament of Holy Baptism and in the support for the baptized that must follow. They can be helped by what Luther said about this sacrament. Divide the class in half. Ask one group to think of ways the first two questions in the Catechism might be used to help sponsors and parents. Ask the other group to think of ways the third and fourth questions might be used similarly. Then have a general discussion.

Baptism and prayer

These discussions can lead to further small group discussion. You may want to talk about how God's promise in Baptism is a part of their own life of prayer. Another topic could be the implications of Baptism in their work and other daily activities. Ask them to pay particular attention to the second and fourth questions in this section of the Small Catechism (study book pages 44, 46).

FOR REFLECTION

The first question under "For Reflection" on page 47 of the study book can follow easily on the small and large group discussions. Those discussions have dealt with the promise and benefits of Baptism from several points of view. This question places the emphasis on the way the learner understands what Luther said. Encourage class members to put the summary into their own words. Try to avoid just a recitation of Luther's words. Keep the emphasis here on the learner's perspective.

The second and third questions also can be answered directly from the ideas generated in the discussions. You might want to use these questions in the discussions during the session.

OUR PRAYERS

The suggestions under "Our Prayers" on page 47 of the study book will build upon what was done in the session with the liturgy for Holy Baptism and on the ideas to help learners explore the meaning of living in their own Baptism. Encourage class members to use their earlier discussion and reflection here in a devotional way. This experience will highlight for them the close interconnection between a life of faith expressed devotionally and a life of faith expressed in the word of belief. You may also want to use one of the Holy Baptism prayers from *Prayers Based on Luther's Small Catechism*.

 ## POST-STUDY

Expanding the session

☐ Establish monthly Baptism anniversary services in the congregation.

☐ Encourage class members to think about other questions from the discussion on Baptism in daily life that were recorded on the chalkboard or newsprint.

☐ Ask the pastor for information on recent Baptisms. Send notes of support and encouragement to parents and sponsors. Perhaps start a sponsors and parents support group using suggestions from the class discussion on ways the four questions in the catechism can help sponsors and parents.

☐ Ask permission to sit in on a Baptism preparation class.

Looking ahead

• If you decide to spend more than one session on this chapter, make clear what will be covered in the next class meeting. Assign any reading from the study book or Bible to help the participants prepare for the next session.

• Read through the parts of the study book and this guide that will be the focus of the next session.

• Decide how you will use the Small Catechism and the commentary in the study book.

• Work through the questions in the commentary and under "For Reflection" and plan which ones you will use.

• Decide which of the "Expanding and Learning" activities you will use or encourage the participants to use.

CHAPTER 5

Food for travelers

FOCUS STATEMENT

In the scriptural accounts of the Lord's Supper, Jesus gave his disciples the food necessary to sustain them on their journey in faith. Moreover, he promised to be with them always wherever that meal was celebrated.

OBJECTIVES

This chapter will help adults:
- receive the Lord's Supper, confident of its gift and promise;
- deepen their awareness of God's grace;
- seek strength through regular participation in the sacrament.

✝ PRE-STUDY

Background: The Sacrament of Holy Communion

In the scriptural accounts of the Lord's Supper (Matthew 26:26-30; Mark 14:22-26; Luke 22:14-23, 1 Corinthians 11:23-26), Jesus gave his disciples the food necessary to sustain them on their journey in faith. Moreover, he promised to be with them always whenever that meal was celebrated. This gift and promise are given again and again in our lives each time we come to the Lord's Supper. Here we receive food for travelers, such as we are in life, in the presence of the risen Christ.

There is a story about a man who bought a donkey. His friends told him he would have to give it a certain amount of food each day. This he thought was too much. He decided to experiment and see if he could get the animal used to less food. Each day he reduced its rations. Eventually the donkey was reduced to almost no food at all and fell over and died. "What a pity," thought the man. "If I had had a little more time, I could have gotten it accustomed to living on nothing at all."

This story says that food is necessary to sustain life under any circumstances. It also suggests that food needs to be taken regularly. In the same way, we need to be nourished by the meal given us by Jesus. We need to take that food regularly lest we come to think that that journey can be sustained on next to nothing.

The journey is at best a challenge and at worst a hazard. There is no use blinking at the fact that weariness and doubt are always present to remind us of the struggles we face to be faithful. Nor can we say with any degree of confidence that we can rid ourselves of the personal desolation brought on by despair.

The demands of the Christian life are rigorous. The journey is filled with daily dying and rising through Baptism until physical death. For all that, we need the grace of Christ offered in the meal he set before his first disciples and continues to set before us in the sacrament we know as the Lord's Supper.

Learning about the sacraments involves two important goals. First, it is important to learn what the sacraments mean, how they have come to us from Christ through the church, and what their purpose is in the Christian life. Second, it is important to learn about our own participation in the sacraments.

The best image for bringing these goals together is that of a journey in faith. A journey has purpose and meaning. It also involves us in the process of living the purpose and meaning. So it is with the sacraments. It is not enough just to know about them and to understand their purpose and meaning. One must participate in them.

Similarly, it is not enough just to go the Lord's Supper and receive it as if it stood completely by itself. The sacraments are visible words, not visible objects. The word of the sacraments binds us to Christ from whom we receive meaning and purpose.

The image of a journey in faith for learning about and participating in the sacraments allows us to see the connection between the effect of what we know on our participation and the effect of our participation on what we know.

For example, when we learn about the Lord's Supper, we hear Christ's command and promise. When we participate in this sacrament, we receive the blessing of this meal—the forgiveness of sins and the strengthening of our faith for the journey of life.

Eating is important because it sustains life. Further, meals are more important because they foster relationships that shape and reshape the meaning of life. Our society doesn't always encourage or even recognize the difference. More often than not, our mealtimes are just refueling activities. How often have you said, "I'm just going to grab a bite to eat"?

Meals are gathering places for family and friends. They can be the settings for conversation and sharing life together. The food associated with them serves as a complement to all that. The joy of taste is enhanced, not just because of spices in the recipe, but because of all the emotions in the relationships that emerge through conversation and sharing.

It is significant that when Jesus gave his disciples food for the journey, he gave it in the context of a meal. Furthermore, this meal was not just an afterthought that could be satisfied at a fast-food restaurant. The meal was a solemn, joyful gathering of family and friends around the celebration of Passover. That setting made all the difference. The food was more than something to eat. It was food connected to what Jesus said in the context of a meal that commemorated God's promise of his steadfast covenant with people. Jesus himself confirmed that covenant the night before he was put to death with those words of promise, "This is my body . . . This is my blood" (Mark 14:22-24).

As in Baptism, Christians can rely on Christ's command and promise in the Lord's Supper. "Do this in remembrance of me," Jesus said after offering both the bread and wine (1 Corinthians 11:25). We are called upon to receive in simple trust the gift of food, believing in the promise that Jesus will be with us and for us.

The promise of Christ goes beyond just his presence. With his presence, Jesus pronounces the free and unmerited forgiveness of sins. The implications of that are far-reaching, beyond this life in fact. The forgiveness of sins is not just wiping away the wrongs we have done. It is a promise that we will also know life and salvation. In the act of forgiveness, our old selves are put to death. In overcoming death, Jesus gave us life now and the hope of resurrection from the dead.

Life and salvation go together because salvation does not only mean being freed or saved *from* something. It means that in the promise of Christ we are freed or saved *for* something. Salvation is not the cancellation of life, but bringing life to its fullness. This means that in the forgiveness of sins, life is meant to be lived. Forgiveness does not involve some kind of trans-

portation into a perfect land. Nor is it the sign of perfection achieved once and for all. Forgiveness allows us to live fully as human partners in the work of God in the world. That partnership takes place where the challenge and hazard of the journey in faith come together, where we constantly need renewal and sustenance in order to go on. That is where this meal is a necessity. This food will not satisfy us forever, but it is the food we need for the moment.

The Lord's Supper reminds us of two things: who Christ is for us and who we are for Christ's sake. Christ conquered death for us and continues to give us new life with him. But we live in this world now, subject to all its limitations, to be Christ's people.

In Romans and 1 Corinthians, Paul called the church the "body of Christ." He used this description to speak about the close relationship between believers and the risen, exalted Lord. "Now you are the body of Christ," Paul wrote in 1 Corinthians 12:27. So are we who gather around the risen, exalted Christ in the Lord's Supper. We are the body of Christ. Paul also recorded the words of Jesus at the Last Supper, "This is my body that is for you" (1 Corinthians 11:24). And so it is for us today. In the Lord's Supper is the body of Christ for you.

Materials needed

Bibles • study books • chalkboard and chalk or newsprint and markers • pens or pencils • writing paper • copies of Lutheran Book of Worship *• one copy of* Prayers Based on Luther's Small Catechism *• "The Lord's Supper and My Journey in Faith" worksheet (see "Before the Study" on page 25) • copies of* Holy Communion Narrative for Adults *(Augsburg Publishing House and Board of Publication of the Lutheran Church in America, 1978) • copies of* A Statement on Communion Practices *(Augsburg Publishing House and Board of Publications of the Lutheran Church in America, 1978).*

Before the study

___ Examine your own understanding of the Lord's Supper. How do your experiences compare with those of others? Be mindful that the chapter wants to encourage a positive understanding of the Christian life and the ways the Lord's Supper can be received.

___ Prepare the worksheet on typing paper. Turn the paper horizontally and title it "The Lord's Supper and My Journey in Faith." Space these questions equally across the top of the page: **1.** *What does the liturgy say about what I will find in my journey in faith?* **2.** *How does the sacrament help me in my journey?* **3.** *What are the things in the liturgy that are most difficult and easiest to apply to my life?* Make one copy for each participant.

___ Speak to your pastor about First Communion practices in your congregation or in your national church. If your congregation has opened the Lord's Supper to all baptized people, what was the process by which it made the decision to do so? Are there experiences from other congregations that could be explored?

___ Talk with people in the altar guild or worship committee to find out about preparation for Communion. Are there training sessions for those who prepare the bread, wine, and other items for Holy Communion? How might others become involved in this service?

 **STUDY**

ENTRY

The purpose of the activity in this section is to introduce the participants to some of the key themes of the Sacrament of Holy Communion and Luther's explanations from the Small Catechism.

Luther's Small Catechism

Ask the participants to locate the opening paragraph that begins on page 48 in their study books. This section begins with the words "Luther's Small Catechism." You may want to ask for a volunteer or two to read aloud this section or have the participants quickly scan it for themselves. You may wish to share some of the following as you discuss this section in the study book.

There are three central ideas in the entry material. The first is the recognition that the Christian life is rigorous and demanding. The second is that we are offered strength in the Lord's Supper to sustain us in this journey of life. The third is the observation that this sacrament has been called by different names, indicating a breadth of understanding of it on the basis of human experience throughout the history of the church. All three ideas are important foundations for leading this session.

The Christian life is rigorous and demanding. This is not to say it is drowned in suffering and sorrow. To call it rigorous and demanding is to place high value on what it represents. It calls for the best from a person and, similarly, offers the best. A life that is rigorous and demanding can be beset by many troublesome risks, but it is fundamentally a positive challenge.

This is the perspective through which the Sacrament of the Lord's Supper views the Christian life. It is a call to journey with Christ in a life of faith that will be sustained through its many difficulties by the grace of God. Learning about this sacrament and participating in it regularly are activities through which God calls us to faith and trust in God's promise to save. It is a journey in faith.

This journey is a series of moments and occasions in which we find strength to go on as we are nourished by the strength of Christ who calls us. It is an "alien" strength in that it comes from outside us—from God. We cannot save ourselves, but God can and does. It is the strength we need, forged in Christ's suffering and death and made available to us as the power of his resurrection (Philippians 3:10) in the bread and wine of his supper.

When we begin thinking and talking about this sacrament, many images come to mind. It is not one-dimensional or specific for only certain life experiences. It has been known and lived in a variety of ways by people who name the name of Christ and throughout the history of the church.

Names identify things, either because of what they are in themselves or because of what they mean to those who experience them. So it is with this sacrament. It has been called by different names in addition to the Lord's Supper—Holy Communion, Eucharist, and the Sacrament of the Altar. In a broad sense, each name helps us know something about this sacrament. Each has its own emphasis.

At this point, explore the names the participants use for this sacrament. Explore their reasons for using the specific name and what they might learn about the sacrament by using other names.

EXPLORING THE STUDY BOOK

Reading the Sacrament of Holy Communion

The purpose of this section is to introduce the participants to the Sacrament of Holy Communion by reading it along with Luther's explanations from the Small Catechism.

Ask the participants to locate Chapter 5, "Food for Travelers," beginning on page 48 in the study book. Point out that the Sacrament of Holy Communion and Luther's explanations are printed in the narrow column throughout the chapter. Have the participants quickly scan the Sacrament of Holy Communion and Luther's explanations. Use the corresponding commentary, discussion questions, and Bible verses in the study book to guide the class discussion.

Key points to consider

• Relate Luther's questions and explanations in this part of the Small Catechism with the part of Holy Baptism. Point out how the two parts say much the same thing.

• Discuss Augustine's saying, "Believe and you have already eaten" (page 51 of the study book). Can the reverse also be said, "Eat and you already believe"?

• Be sure to discuss with the participants the matter of preparation for the Lord's Supper (Question 4 of this part of the Small Catechism). See page 52 of the study book.

DIGGING DEEPER

Liturgy of the Lord's Supper

As in the session on "From Death to Life" (Chapter 4), use the liturgy in *Lutheran Book of Worship* as a focus. Select one of the three settings for Holy Communion, perhaps the one currently in use in your congregation. Point out that although the whole Sunday morning liturgy is called "Holy Communion," the specific part that deals with the administration of the sacrament begins with the Great Thanksgiving, (*LBW*, page 68) and concludes with the dismissal of the congregation.

"The Lord's Supper and My Journey in Faith" worksheet

Distribute copies of the worksheet "The Lord's Supper and My Journey in Faith" to the participants. Be sure they have copies of *Lutheran Book of Worship*. Have each person write his or her own responses to the questions. Then divide the class into groups of three or four for discussion of these worksheets. Following this small group discussion, have a general discussion centering around the conversations in the small groups and list on a chalkboard or newsprint the different kinds of responses made.

Using the liturgy this way reinforces its Sunday morning use and will help class members apply its meaning to their life situations week after week. This activity will also prepare for the next consideration, the connection between participating in the sacrament and understanding it.

This connection is an important one to explore in order for class members to see how this sacrament effects their lives. Perhaps the easier and less threatening way to do this will be to have a discussion in the whole class: first about experiences of participating in the Lord's Supper, followed by talk about how members understand it. Be prepared to start a list on the chalkboard or newsprint as you take up the next activities.

Early experiences with the Lord's Supper

Encourage the class to recall some of their first experiences of participating in the Lord's Supper. What were these experiences like? How are they different from more recent experiences? Who else was part of these experiences?

Ask what different ways they have participated in the Lord's Supper. Have any been assisting ministers or communion assistants? Have any helped with home communions? Have any served on altar guilds and been responsible for communion?

Encourage comments on changes class members have noticed in the ways people have participated in communion over the years. That will serve as a transition to talk about what members understand about the Lord's Supper.

Four questions

Ask the participants to turn to the commentary in the study book. Divide the class into four groups. Try to have at least two people in each group. Assign groups one of the four questions in the Catechism and commentary. If you have a small class, divide into two groups and assign two questions to each group. Ask group members to discuss together their experiences of participating in the Lord's Supper. Ask the groups to list agreements and disagreements and report back to the whole class. After each has reported to the class, turn to the next activity, a personal statement of understanding about the Lord's Supper.

Ask members to briefly write or tell another person what the Lord's Supper means to them, putting together both the experience of participating in it and what they have come to understand about it. This should be their personal statements that can serve them in their journey in faith in the church. As individuals care to, let them share these statements with the class.

Options for further study

As time permits, other ideas can be explored: participation as personal witness, other names for the Lord's Supper, events in a meal compared with the communion liturgy (using the *Holy Communion Narrative for Adults* booklet), first communion practices in the ELCA (using *A Statement on Communion Practices*).

FOR REFLECTION

The first two questions under "For Reflection" on page 53 of the study book can be used in connection with the personal statement on communion. The third question can pick up discussion earlier on either experiences of participation or experiences of understanding.

OUR PRAYERS

Supplement the suggestions in "Our Prayers" on page 53 of the study book with one or two communion hymns. Let the class members select the hymns used. You may want to refer to "Topical Index of Hymns" on pages 932–939 of *Lutheran Book of Worship*. Use a Holy Communion prayer from *Prayers Based on Luther's Small Catechism*.

POST-STUDY

Expanding the session

☐ Suggest that the questions on the worksheets can be used in other settings with friends or family members to explore together experiences of the Lord's Supper and how these inform one's journey in faith.

The process of going from experiences of participation to understanding to personal statement of faith can be used by mentors with youth in confirmation classes.

☐ This session might be the basis for encouraging further study of the practice of communion in your congregation, either through the worship committee or a study group. There might be opportunities through the worship committee to use the *Holy Communion Narrative for Adults* in the Sunday morning worship service.

☐ If there are items from the general discussion of the liturgy worksheets that were not dealt with, ask the class to reflect further on them during the coming week.

☐ Encourage members to volunteer to assist with Holy Communion. Put them in touch with the worship committee or pastor. There might be opportunities for providing transportation for home communions, especially during festival seasons of the church year.

Looking ahead

• If you decide to spend more than one session on this chapter, make clear what will be covered in the next class meeting. Assign any reading from the study book or Bible to help the participants prepare for the next session.

• Read through the parts of the study book and this guide that will be the focus of the next session.

• Decide how you will use the Small Catechism and commentary in the study book.

• Work through the questions in the commentary and under "For Reflection" and plan which ones you will use.

• Decide which of the "Expanding the Learning" activities you will use or encourage the participants to use.

CHAPTER 6

Going it together

FOCUS STATEMENT

The church is the fellowship in which believers walk together with God. It, too, is active and dynamic, growing and changing. It is characterized by a variety of relationships in which believers discover the richness of faith. It is a place of rest but not a permanent shelter. We are never finally secure from the hazards and risks of life in the world.

OBJECTIVES

This chapter will help adults:
- know what Luther said about the believing Christian and the nature of the church and the relationship between the two;
- grow in and share with others the experience of trust in God;
- discover new ways to walk the journey of faith with other Christians in the presence of God.

 **PRE-STUDY**

Background: Seven Marks of the Church

Living the faith is a matter of relationships. At the very least, it is a relationship between two, the believer and God. Beyond that, relationships are limited only by the capacity of each person to maintain them. Faith is never experienced in isolation. There are no solitary Christians. Being a Christian means membership in the church, the body of Christ, where faith is trust in God's decision to save us without merit. In this light, the faith we receive from God is bound up with the faith of others.

Faith is first of all a gift of God. It is also walking in the journey of life with others in the presence of God. Moreover, the relationships that are part of that walk are active and dynamic. They depend on who we are and what we share in supporting and influencing each other.

Even at times when we may feel far from God, we have the assurance that God has not abandoned us. It is the role of other Christians to remind us of God's presence to speak the gospel to us over and over again, to keep us in fellowship with one another and with the God who saves. Through God's Word and in fellowship with one another, we can be rescued from times of unbelief and despair. In the same way, through the Word and other people, we can celebrate God's promise to save.

The prayer, "Gracious Lord, through water and the Spirit," in the service for Affirmation of Baptism (*LBW*, page 201) says that God brought us to newness of life through water and the Spirit. The prayer asks that God will continue to strengthen us with the Holy Spirit and daily increase in us the gifts of grace. In this service we pray for "the spirit of wisdom and understanding, the spirit of counsel and might, the spirit of knowledge and the fear of the Lord, the spirit of joy in your [God's] presence" (*LBW*, page 201). This strength and the increase of the gifts of grace come to us from God through the community of faith, the church.

The church is the fellowship in which believers walk together with God. It, too, is active and dynamic, growing and changing. It is characterized by a variety of relationships in which believers discover the richness of faith. It is a place of rest but not a permanent shelter. We are never finally secure from the hazards and risks of life in the world.

When we live in the church, we never stop growing or changing. On the contrary, living in the church means being challenged to grow and change in ways undreamed of in the world. As the prayer at the end of the Holy Communion service says, we pray that God "would strengthen us, through this gift, in faith toward you [God] and in fervent love toward one another" (*LBW*, page 74).

This strength comes from listening to and hearing the Word of God and is accompanied by six other marks or characteristics of the church described in the study book: Baptism, the Lord's Supper, confession and absolution, the ministry, worship, and suffering. The chapter title "Going It Together" evokes an image of the church as walking and being with God and fellow believers for strengthening through the Holy Spirit and the increase of the gifts and grace.

The seven marks of the church are circular in their relationship. Each stands in its own right and is, at the same time, related to all others. Together, they are like points on a compass. In their independence and interdependence they all presuppose each other. It is hard to place these seven marks in order of importance. One can find in the history of the church and in contemporary discussions suggestions for a ranking or a selection of two or three marks that are held to be the foundation for the others. But as soon as one tries to build an argument for priority, the ranking quickly dissolves into a circle again. One cannot speak about the sacraments, for example, without referring to the Word of God, or the Word of God without referring to the ministry and proclamation, or confession and absolution without referring to suffering and worship.

Given the circular relationship of the marks of the church, one nevertheless usually begins to talk about these marks with the one that seems most important in a given situation. From there, conversation inevitably leads to the other marks.

Each mark is a way of designating and dealing with what is of importance in a specific situation and, at the same time, is a point of entry into the whole circle and into the richness of meaning the whole circle gives to the individual marks.

In the discussion that follows, we will look at each of the seven marks in the order given in the study book and consider their educational implications.

The Word of God. The Word of God means several things, all of which go back to the root meaning of "word" as that which is spoken and heard. But in the way Luther referred to the Word of God, it is clear that speaking and hearing were not limited to their literal meanings. The Word of God comes in many ways. God spoke, and all creation came about. We must be attentive to God's creating word, embrace it, and hold it fast.

God "spoke" also in Jesus Christ, the Word that became flesh (John 1:1-5, 10-18). We must be attentive to what Jesus literally said and to what he did.

God's word is also in the words of Scripture. In Scripture is the story of faith that God's people tell from generation to generation, that they gather to hear again and again in the company of the faithful, and that they are given faith to believe in their hearts.

Baptism. Luther emphasized the connection of the Word of God with the water of Baptism. In so doing, he pointed out that, although the visible sign in the sacrament is important, we cannot make it the center of our teaching. Water and the Word are instruments through which God's grace comes to us.

In this sacrament of Holy Baptism, we die to our old selves and are raised again to new life in Christ (Romans 6:1-4). We participate in the saving act of God in Christ and become members of the church. Baptism is the sign of who we are. People are not born Christian. People become Christians by the gift of God through Baptism.

Baptism reminds all who see it that the church is present and the journey of faith with others takes place in the presence of God.

The Lord's Supper. This sacrament is a sign of the unity of the church as it brings the grace of God to believers. It is the forgiveness of sins and reconciliation. Like Baptism, the Lord's Supper is not just the bread and wine but the Word of God that unites, forgives, and reconciles.

In practice, this sacrament is the one more closely associated with Jesus' life. When we teach about this sacrament, we speak directly and concretely about the gospel. In so doing, we relate this food for faith given to us by the suffering of Christ to our suffering as a mark of the church.

Confession and absolution. These marks of the church are public acts in several respects. They are never private experiences like the inner conversations we sometimes have with ourselves. They always involve someone else, a representative of the community, someone who serves the gospel and us as more than a close friend. This person has the authority to speak and pronounce forgiveness in the name of Christ. In addition, these marks are public in the sense that they have their source in God. God calls us to confession. It is from God alone that we receive absolution (forgiveness of sin).

We confess our sins to God in a community of faith. This means that even in private prayer we are surrounded by the faithful. This also means that it is good and right to confess to God in the hearing and physical presence of the faithful. The faithful serve not only as support and company for the act of confession. They are also a source of assurance of the forgiveness of God.

In the exchange of confession and absolution is the reminder to each other of the seriousness with which we must view our life before God and our responsibilities toward each other in the community of faith. That seriousness and responsibility have binding effects as we make them known to each other. They are critical elements in what we teach and learn about our journey together before God in the church.

The ministry. Ministers are storytellers, tellers of the gospel story. That includes everyone in the church from the youngest to the oldest. That also means the story will be told in a variety of ways—with words, signs, and gestures.

Yet, as a very practical matter, it is not possible for everyone to be a storyteller in the church at the same time or even for everyone to take turns being the representative storyteller for the community. Neither are all people given the gifts necessary. Storytellers have a function to perform in service of the gospel, and the community of faith has the responsibility to designate those who will fulfill that function. These gifted people have been called by the church and the Holy Spirit to be pastors.

Pastors are servants of the Word and sacraments of God and caretakers of the flock of God. They do the public work of ministry. As the church receives that ministry, it is encouraged by the gospel and, in turn, encourages and supports the ones called to this important ministry.

Worship. In its broadest sense, worship is a way of life. It has to do with what we do in the journey of faith and how we do it. It is the way we express what we believe. The study book points out that we worship God in telling the story of Jesus, in prayer, and in our praise of God.

Worship bears the message of salvation in word, song, and action. It is a drama of faith for those who desire to know Jesus Christ. It also gathers up the beliefs of Christians down through the ages and gives them a setting in the contemporary world. It is a picture of the journey in faith that countless believers have taken.

From worship, believers go out to serve in the world. That service takes many forms, but its central thrust is the gospel that calls Christians to honor God and to live their faith for the sake of others.

Suffering. The inevitability of suffering in this life, for reasons that are as mysterious as they are many, is paralleled only by the certainty of Christ's victory over suffering and death and by our claim to be part of that victory. The gospel is not pessimistic. It is simply realistic. It knows the depths we all experience. It knows our limitations and the power of evil. And it also knows that even the last enemy, death, will not be able to separate us from the love of God in Christ.

Note: In this reprint edition, the poster has been discontinued.

Materials needed

Bibles • study books • "Seven Marks of the Church" poster • chalkboard and chalk or newsprint and markers • pens or pencils • writing paper • copies of Lutheran Book of Worship *• one copy of* Prayers Based on Luther's Small Catechism *• large candle • building blocks (Legos™ or Tinkertoys™) • modeling clay • "What Does It Take?" worksheets (see "Before the Study" below).*

Before the study

___ Prepare the worksheet "What Does It Take?" Put that title at the top of a sheet of typing paper. Make one copy for each participant for use under "Digging Deeper."

___ Remove "Seven Marks of the Church" poster from the center of this guide and display it prominently in your class area.

___ Read the constitution of your congregation to find out how the church is defined there for comparison with Luther's seven characteristic marks of the church.

___ Take an informal survey among members of the congregation you know well on what they think about the relationship between personal faith and communal faith.

___ Make a list of ways your congregation manifests "Going It Together."

___ Go over earlier chapters on Baptism, the Lord's Supper, and the Apostles' Creed in this guide and in the study book.

✠ STUDY

ENTRY

The purpose of the activities in this section is to introduce the participants to some of the key themes of the seven marks of the church—the Word, Baptism, the Lord's Supper, confession and absolution, the ministry, worship, and suffering.

Faith is

Ask the participants to locate "Faith Is" on page 55 in their study books. You may want to ask for a volunteer or two to read aloud this section or have the participants quickly scan it for themselves.

This chapter is about having faith and living it in the community of believers. The opening paragraphs on pages 55-56 in the study book state clearly that these are fundamentally related issues. It points to both the personal and communal character of the Christian faith.

The best way to help the class realize this interrelationship is to have participants explore each mark of the church separately first and then see how the interrelationship works in life.

Personal faith is usually a very private matter. Most often that privacy comes out of a desire to know one's own religious identity and experience the depth of one's beliefs. Sometimes privacy is also a way of guarding against embarrassment. Therefore, ask class members to make a list of the things they believe as Christians and to place them in order of importance. Keep these lists for further reference.

What do Christians believe?

Engage the class in a general discussion about what Christians believe. Make a list of things proposed on a chalkboard or newsprint sheet.

After this discussion, ask class members to individually reflect on connections they see between their personal list and the group list compiled under "Faith Is . . ." above.

These connections can be the basis for further exploration. For example, encourage the class to think about the ways personal and communal faith influence each other and how they can be sources for mutual learning and growth.

Growth can mean the positive development and enrichment of what one already believes and does or a corrective challenge to those beliefs and behaviors. By encouraging discussion, you will be able to raise the matter of church membership—what it means to individuals and how the definition of church from Luther's seven characteristic marks shapes an individual's understanding of membership.

EXPLORING THE STUDY BOOK

Seven marks of the church

The purpose of this section is to introduce the participants to what Luther called the seven marks or characteristics of the church. This section in this chapter is different from the other "Reading the . . ." sections under "Exploring the Study Book" in the previous five chapters of the study book. These seven marks of the church are not part of Luther's Small Catechism, but they are very evident throughout Luther's explanations in the Catechism.

Ask the participants to locate Chapter 6, "Going It Together," beginning on page 55 in the study book. Detach "Seven Marks of the Church" poster from the center of this guide. Display it where all can see it. Have the participants locate these marks and the commentary about them in the study book beginning on page 56. (Note that Baptism and the Lord's Supper are discussed in the same section.) Use the images on the poster, the corresponding commentary, discussion questions, and Bible verses below each section in the study book to guide the class discussion.

Key points to consider

• Although the seven marks of the church are interdependent, help the participants see that an understanding of the Word of God is very important to fully understand the other six marks of the church. Review together the commentary on the Word of God on page 56 of the study book.

Point out that the Word of God is not only the Bible, but it is first of all Jesus Christ himself—God's Word made flesh among us. You may want to read aloud John 1:1-5, 10-18.

• Use "The Office of the Keys" and "Confession" from Luther's Small Catechism that are printed on page 64 of the study book when discussing the mark of confession and absolution. Point out that all Christians are called to speak God's word of forgiveness to one another in Jesus' name. It is not necessary that the one speaking forgiveness be an ordained minister.

• Many people have deep questions about suffering. Be sure to spend time reading and discussing the section on suffering on pages 60-61 in the study book. You may also want to consult other Christian books on suffering such as *Where Is God in My Suffering? Biblical Responses to Seven Searching Questions* by Daniel J. Simundson (Augsburg, 1983).

DIGGING DEEPER

"What Does It Take?" worksheet

Following the discussion directions under "Entry" above will help you to prepare for using the "What Does It Take?" worksheet in this session. Distribute worksheets to the participants. Ask participants to write down or draw what they see as being essential for an organization to call itself a church. They may list visible items such as building, leaders, or the Bible. They may also list invisible items such as faith, trust, commitment, and love. Allow about three or four minutes for participants to make their lists. When they have finished, divide the class into groups of three and ask them to share their responses and to be ready to report common agreements and disagreements to the whole class. When the groups share their responses, make lists on the chalkboard of the agreements and disagreements.

Then, ask the class to get into the same groups of three and discuss what each person does with agreements and disagreements, and how those things affect their experience of the community of faith.

Go back to the chapters on Baptism, the Lord's Supper, and the Apostles' Creed and review suggestions in them that could be used in studying faith and the sacraments. There may be material you did not cover in those chapters that could be used here.

Building on faith

The journey in faith produces an image of building and construction. As in the first session, encourage art as a means of expression. Have available clay for modeling, building blocks, sheets of writing paper and pens or pencils, and sheets of newsprint with felt pens for drawing. Ask class members to select one of the art materials to construct or draw their interpretation of the church as a community of faith.

Special reports

Determine if there is special interest among class members for one or two marks of the church. Put together those with similar interests and ask them to share with the class on what they think is important about the mark they choose.

Another way to do this activity is to ask class members to explain what they understand about the seven marks of the church from their experience. Use the discussion about the seven marks of the church being circular in their relationship (pages 28-29 in this guide) as a resource for the class.

You could also have each class member tell a personal or family story of an experience in the church to one other person, pointing out the parts that were most significant for him or her.

FOR REFLECTION

The first question under "For Reflection" on page 63 of the study book could be easily used as a follow-up to the discussion about marks of the church. Class members might have already talked about what needs to be added to or left out of the list of seven characteristics.

The crucial item in the second question is the criteria in Luther's understanding for determining variety in forms and practices of the church. Identifying criteria is crucial because there are not many stated restrictions. And yet, freedom is not without guidelines and limits. Preaching the gospel and administering the sacraments are central

to Luther's understanding of the church. Both always need definition in any conversation.

The third question can be dealt with as a Bible study on the two passages of Scripture mentioned.

OUR PRAYERS

The focus in "Our Prayers" on page 63 in the study book is upon prayer. Light a candle as a focal point for worship. As a class, pray the "Prayer of the Church" aloud (LBW, pages 52-53). Divide the class into two groups and have the groups pray it responsively as a sign of shared life in the community. You may also want to select a prayer from Prayers Based on Luther's Small Catechism that fits one or more of the seven marks of the church as discussed in this chapter.

 **POST-STUDY**

Expanding the session

☐ Invite a hospital or nursing home chaplain to speak with your class about the role God's Word plays in bringing hope, healing, and comfort to those who are sick or dying.

☐ Make seven banners, each one representing a mark of the church. Display them in your congregation's worship space.

☐ With your pastor and worship committee, plan and institute a service of confession and absolution. You may want to use the service "Corporate Confession and Forgiveness" (LBW, pages 193-195).

☐ Tour your church building or that of another congregation to see how the seven marks of the church are evident in the architecture and decorations of the building.

Looking ahead

• If you decide to spend more than one session on this chapter, make clear what will be covered in the next class meeting. Assign any reading from the study book or Bible to help the participants prepare for the next session.

• Read through the parts of the study book and this guide that will be the focus of the next session.

• Decide how you will use the Small Catechism and commentary on the seven marks of the church.

• Work through the questions in the commentary and under "For Reflection" and plan which ones you will use.

• Decide which of the "Expanding the Learning" activities you will use or encourage the participants to use.